To Liz

My inspiration and beautiful friend

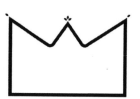

TABLE OF CONTENTS

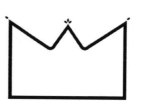

ACKNOWLEDGMENTS

First and foremost, I thank God for placing this project on my heart. He has shown me the delight of collaboration and given me the gift of His creativity expressed through His children. He is so good!

Thank you Liz, for being your beautiful self. We are all drawn to your beauty, and I'm grateful for your support from the very beginning.

Thank you Anna, for allowing me to use your gorgeous photos for the book cover and for my website. You have perfectly captured the beauty of God.

Thank you Hope, for sharing your artistic talents which allows us time to slow down and express our creativity in a joyful way.

Thank you Rebecca, for sharing your musical gifts and for making *You Are Beautiful* come alive.

Thank you Micah, for your expertise in recording *You Are Beautiful* and for believing in the message.

Thank you Jose, for your encouragement and for sacrificing precious time during your busy camp season to score *You Are Beautiful*.

Thank you Haley, for creatively compiling this project with your photography and design, business acumen, and enthusiasm for the vision of *You Are Beautiful*.

Thank you Rebecka, for being my cheerleader throughout the project. Your positive outlook and help with business details continue to be greatly appreciated!

Thank you Fritzeen, for always being there for me whenever I call and for sharing your godly wisdom. You are truly my spiritual rock!

And lastly, to my biggest and constant supporter, David, I thank you from the bottom of my heart. I thank you for believing in me to turn this project into a reality, for showing me how to selflessly love others with the love of Christ, and for displaying the beauty of God's love every day. I love you!

My most sincere gratitude to you all! Without you, *The Beautiful Project* would simply not exist.

8

INTRODUCTION

I thank God you have decided to take this 40 day journey;
a journey that will help bring you from any darkness of deception into the glorious light of truth.

HISTORY

What began as a simple song to encourage a friend, has made its way to becoming a journal and is now in your hands.

The song, *You Are Beautiful*, speaks to the attributes of who we are in Christ, as we surrender ourselves and put our faith in the redeeming power of the cross. It reveals true beauty is God's love being poured out of us from His Spirit. When this love overflows it displays itself as physical beauty. In a time where outward beauty is so highly valued, we can be overwhelmed by feeling less than the airbrushed models we see in magazines or the starving actresses we see on screen. The feeling of insecurity is real, but it's just a feeling. The Truth is: you are beautiful! Most importantly, your beauty is from the inside and will not fade.

One day, I was reflecting on how the song had blessed my friend. In that time of thanking the Holy Spirit for using me to minister to her, I began to think of John 10:10: "The thief comes only in order to steal and kill and destroy. I came that they may have and enjoy life, and have it in abundance [to the full, till it overflows]" (Amplified Bible).

I stared in the face of that truth and pondered the power of this revelation in my own life. The thief had stolen from me, killed those dear to me, and tried to destroy me several times, and yet, I am living a victorious life: the life that Jesus died to give me. It is not a perfect life, but rather, an imperfect one. I rely on my Savior every single day for everything I need.

Through my own experiences the Spirit showed me how the thief has waged war on women. Many are losing the battle. Strong and determined women, who love God and want to fulfill their destiny, are powerless if they are living a life in deception. I sensed something rising up in me, and was certain God wanted me to help make a difference.

The next thing I knew, the Spirit whispered the idea of combining the song with a journal for women. With 40 lines in the song, it could make for a 40 day journal. Each day the participant would focus on just one line of the song, allowing time for contemplation of God's Truth. The 40 days would become a journey with God and the Spirit as He lovingly shares His Truth and silences the lies of the enemy. It's the last thing I thought I'd ever do, and yet you are now holding that very journal.

9

LIES VS. TRUTH

We all share the experience of having believed a lie, and the destruction it caused in our lives. Even though we may have heard Truth and know it in our minds, we may still believe the lies. Some lies are buried deep within us. Some of us hold on to the lies for years, and so the destruction follows for years: *You are not good enough. You can't do that. You're not smart enough. You are only accepted when you are perfect. It was your fault. You need to try harder. You're not normal like everybody else.* These are examples of the destructive lies women live with everyday.

These lies become more dangerous when they move from a thought in our minds to a belief in our hearts. Once the lie becomes a belief, the enemy uses it to steal, kill, and destroy us. He steals our dreams and destiny, kills our self worth, and destroys our relationships. But Jesus came to give us life! He came in grace and Truth (John 1:17), and that Truth sets us free (John 8:32). We are free from the lies and their destructive power. He desires us to walk in newness of life, in freedom, and with the knowledge of our true identity in Christ (Romans 6:4).

THE 40 DAY JOURNEY

Everyone will have a different 40 day journey experience. For some, it will build self confidence, while for others it may confirm what you already believe, and yet, for others, it will be life changing. There is no right or wrong, nor any expectations. This is *your* 40 day journey.

As I began putting the journal together, I thought I'd have a friend go through the 40 day journey first. She could go through the process, be blessed by what God would reveal to her, and provide me feedback. Yet the Spirit once again whispered to me, "I want *you* to go through the 40 day journey first." Me? But I already know who I am in Christ. I am fine. I don't need to go through this 40 day journey. Boy, had I been deceived! I did need to go through the journey. The enemy tried to steal this blessing away from me before it began. I love my Lord, and in obedience to His will, I started my 40 day journey on June 12, 2016.

On Day 1, the Lord brought me to a passage of scripture I had never seen before. There, in those words, He revealed a wound from a lie that I thought had already been healed. And at the same time, the words described my life as if they were written just for me. Only God and His Truth have such power. The only thing I could write that first day was, "I feel overwhelmed, and I don't use that word lightly. I must read these words again and again today." By the end of my 40 day journey, God had revealed painful truth, healed my wounds, and set me on my path to fulfill my destiny. I then understood why I had to be first; so I would fully know the power of the 40 day journey.

WHY 40 DAYS?

It is not by coincidence the song has 40 lines, and the number 40 has great significance in the Bible. The number 40 can represent a time of trial, testing, and transformation. Jesus was tested in the desert for 40 days. When tempted by the enemy, Jesus showed us how to defeat the enemy – with Truth of the Word (Matthew 4:1-11). The story of Moses displays how we are transformed in the presence of God. For 40 days, Moses met with God on Mount Sinai. When he returned to his people, his face was glowing with the glory of the Lord, so much so, he had to cover it with a veil (Exodus 34:28). Spending 40 days in the presence of God, listening as He speaks to your heart, will transform you. How could it not?

WHAT IS SELAH?

Selah is a Biblical term found in the Psalms. It means, "Stop, think, and ponder these things." This is a very important part of the 40 day journey: to stop, think and ponder about what the truth means to you. Do you believe it? Why do you or don't you? Are you believing a lie instead of the Truth? There is a process that happens between your head and your heart. *Don't rush the process.* If this journey is going to have any impact on your life, you must stop, think and ponder.

HOW TO USE THE 40 DAY JOURNAL

While this journey will be different for each person, here are some ideas that will help create the best experience:

- Pray before beginning each new day. Invite the Lord to clear your mind so that you may hear His voice as He reveals Truth to your heart. It may be difficult, but stay with it. He is with you.

- After prayer, listen to the song, *You Are Beautiful.* You can find it on my website *YouAreBeautifulSelah.com/song*

- Read that day's verse, and ponder it in your heart. Answer the question "What do I believe about this truth?" There are no expectations. There are no right or wrong answers, just honest ones.

- Spend time with God, so you can enter into His presence and hear Him. This time will look different for everyone. How does God speak to you? In prayer? In worship? In scripture? In creation? In dance? In artistic expression? Write your answer here: _____

_____

- After spending time with God, reflect on the Truth He revealed to you in your journal. What did He say? Do you believe Him?

- Write a prayer for the day. If you need help believing His Truth, ask the Spirit to help you receive.

- Use the Creative Pages section of the journal as you wish. You may want to color each day, at the end of a 5 day section, at the end of the 40 days, or not at all. The decision is yours.

- Commitment to 40 consecutive days is key! Jesus did not take a day off in the desert. Moses did not tell God, "Not today God, I'll be back tomorrow." 40 days is significant. I remember feeling ill on day 31, so I came to God, prayed, and wrote in my journal, "I do not feel well physically, neck and head pain, fatigue. Holy Spirit, I come against the enemy and his devious ways. May You restore my health and keep me living in Your freedom today." The point is, I didn't write answers in my journal like it's designed, but I came to God, prayed a short prayer, and made an honest entry on day 31. No guilt, no condemnation, just respecting the journey with honesty.

- Review John 10:10 and keep this Truth in your heart during the 40 days.

- Know that I'm praying for you daily. You may also want to ask your trusted prayer warriors to pray for you as well.

- This journal is meant to be used more than once. Our life is a journey, ever changing as He leads us through ups and downs. The enemy will always try to deceive you, so this 40 day journey will help in times of trial.

MY PRAYER FOR YOU

Dear Heavenly Father, I come to you today with thanksgiving in my heart for who You are and for loving us with a perfect love. As this precious woman embarks on her 40 day journey, I pray that she stands courageous with You by her side as she defeats every lie and deception she currently believes. I pray for commitment, honesty, and revelation of Your Truth, so that she will walk in true freedom that You died to give her. In the Holy and Blessed Name of Jesus, Amen.

My 40 Day Journey

14

You are beautiful
Daughter of the King
Loved above all things
You are beautiful
Yes, you are beautiful

DAY 1
"You are beautiful"

What do I believe about this TRUTH?

_____

_____

_____

_____

_____

_____

_____

_____

_____

_____

_____

_____

_____

_____

_____

_____

_____

_____

_____

_____

_____

_____

What is my response to the revelation of HIS TRUTH?

_____

_____

_____

_____

_____

_____

_____

_____

_____

_____

_____

_____

Today's prayer:

_____

_____

_____

_____

_____

_____

_____

DAY 2
"Daughter of the King"

What do I believe about this TRUTH?

_____

_____

_____

_____

_____

_____

_____

_____

_____

_____

_____

_____

_____

_____

_____

_____

_____

_____

_____

_____

_____

What is my response to the revelation of HIS TRUTH?

_____

_____

_____

_____

_____

_____

_____

_____

_____

_____

_____

_____

Today's prayer:

_____

_____

_____

_____

_____

_____

_____

DAY 3
"Loved above all things"

What do I believe about this TRUTH?

_____

_____

_____

_____

_____

_____

_____

_____

_____

_____

_____

_____

_____

_____

_____

_____

_____

_____

_____

_____

_____

What is my response to the revelation of HIS TRUTH?

_____

_____

_____

_____

_____

_____

_____

_____

_____

_____

_____

Today's prayer:

_____

_____

_____

_____

_____

_____

_____

"You are beautiful"

What do I believe about this TRUTH?

_____

_____

_____

_____

_____

_____

_____

_____

_____

_____

_____

_____

_____

_____

_____

_____

_____

_____

_____

_____

_____

_____

What is my response to the revelation of HIS TRUTH?

_____

_____

_____

_____

_____

_____

_____

_____

_____

_____

_____

_____

Today's prayer:

_____

_____

_____

_____

_____

_____

_____

DAY 5
"Yes, you are beautiful"

What do I believe about this TRUTH?

_____

_____

_____

_____

_____

_____

_____

_____

_____

_____

_____

_____

_____

_____

_____

_____

_____

_____

_____

_____

_____

What is my response to the revelation of HIS TRUTH?

_____

_____

_____

_____

_____

_____

_____

_____

_____

_____

_____

_____

Today's prayer: _____

_____

_____

_____

_____

_____

_____

26

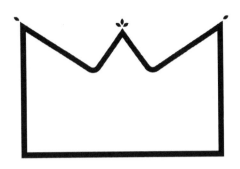

You are lovely
Clothed in His majesty
Yet you wear humilty
You are lovely
And you are beautiful

DAY 6
"You are lovely"

What do I believe about this TRUTH?

_____

_____

_____

_____

_____

_____

_____

_____

_____

_____

_____

_____

_____

_____

_____

_____

_____

_____

_____

_____

_____

What is my response to the revelation of HIS TRUTH?

_____

_____

_____

_____

_____

_____

_____

_____

_____

_____

_____

_____

Today's prayer:

_____

_____

_____

_____

_____

_____

_____

DAY 7
"Clothed in His majesty"

What do I believe about this TRUTH?

_____

_____

_____

_____

_____

_____

_____

_____

_____

_____

_____

_____

_____

_____

_____

_____

_____

_____

_____

_____

What is my response to the revelation of HIS TRUTH?

_____

_____

_____

_____

_____

_____

_____

_____

_____

_____

_____

_____

Today's prayer:

_____

_____

_____

_____

_____

_____

_____

DAY 8
"Yet you wear humility"

What do I believe about this TRUTH?

_____

_____

_____

_____

_____

_____

_____

_____

_____

_____

_____

_____

_____

_____

_____

_____

_____

_____

_____

_____

_____

_____

What is my response to the revelation of HIS TRUTH?

_____

_____

_____

_____

_____

_____

_____

_____

_____

_____

_____

_____

_____

Today's prayer: _____

_____

_____

_____

_____

_____

_____

_____

_____

DAY 9
"You are lovely"

What do I believe about this TRUTH?

_____

_____

_____

_____

_____

_____

_____

_____

_____

_____

_____

_____

_____

_____

_____

_____

_____

_____

_____

_____

_____

What is my response to the revelation of HIS TRUTH?

_____

_____

_____

_____

_____

_____

_____

_____

_____

_____

_____

_____

Today's prayer:

_____

_____

_____

_____

_____

_____

_____

DAY 10
"And you are beautiful"

What do I believe about this TRUTH?

_____

_____

_____

_____

_____

_____

_____

_____

_____

_____

_____

_____

_____

_____

_____

_____

_____

_____

_____

_____

What is my response to the revelation of HIS TRUTH?

_____

_____

_____

_____

_____

_____

_____

_____

_____

_____

_____

_____

Today's prayer:

_____

_____

_____

_____

_____

_____

_____

38

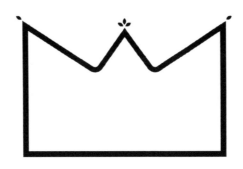

You are joyful
Your spirit's been set free
Grace has brought you peace
You are joyful
And you are beautiful

What do I believe about this TRUTH?

_____

_____

_____

_____

_____

_____

_____

_____

_____

_____

_____

_____

_____

_____

_____

_____

_____

_____

_____

_____

_____

What is my response to the revelation of HIS TRUTH?

_____

_____

_____

_____

_____

_____

_____

_____

_____

_____

_____

_____

_____

Today's prayer:

_____

_____

_____

_____

_____

_____

_____

DAY 12
"Your spirit's been set free"

What do I believe about this TRUTH?

_____

_____

_____

_____

_____

_____

_____

_____

_____

_____

_____

_____

_____

_____

_____

_____

_____

_____

_____

_____

_____

"Your spirit's been set free"

What is my response to the revelation of HIS TRUTH?

_____

_____

_____

_____

_____

_____

_____

_____

_____

_____

_____

_____

Today's prayer: _____

_____

_____

_____

_____

_____

_____

What do I believe about this TRUTH?

_____

_____

_____

_____

_____

_____

_____

_____

_____

_____

_____

_____

_____

_____

_____

_____

_____

_____

_____

_____

_____

_____

What is my response to the revelation of HIS TRUTH?

_____

_____

_____

_____

_____

_____

_____

_____

_____

_____

_____

_____

Today's prayer: _____

_____

_____

_____

_____

_____

_____

_____

What do I believe about this TRUTH?

_____

_____

_____

_____

_____

_____

_____

_____

_____

_____

_____

_____

_____

_____

_____

_____

_____

_____

_____

_____

_____

What is my response to the revelation of HIS TRUTH?

_____

_____

_____

_____

_____

_____

_____

_____

_____

_____

_____

_____

Today's prayer:

_____

_____

_____

_____

_____

_____

_____

What do I believe about this TRUTH?

_____

_____

_____

_____

_____

_____

_____

_____

_____

_____

_____

_____

_____

_____

_____

_____

_____

_____

_____

_____

What is my response to the revelation of HIS TRUTH?

_____

_____

_____

_____

_____

_____

_____

_____

_____

_____

_____

_____

_____

Today's prayer:

_____

_____

_____

_____

_____

_____

_____

50

You are royalty
You wear the victor's crown
Heaven's glow from you abounds
You are royalty
And you are beautiful

What do I believe about this TRUTH?

_____

_____

_____

_____

_____

_____

_____

_____

_____

_____

_____

_____

_____

_____

_____

_____

_____

_____

_____

_____

_____

What is my response to the revelation of HIS TRUTH?

_____

_____

_____

_____

_____

_____

_____

_____

_____

_____

_____

_____

_____

Today's prayer:

_____

_____

_____

_____

_____

_____

_____

"You wear the victor's crown"

What do I believe about this TRUTH?

_____

_____

_____

_____

_____

_____

_____

_____

_____

_____

_____

_____

_____

_____

_____

_____

_____

_____

_____

_____

What is my response to the revelation of HIS TRUTH?

_____

_____

_____

_____

_____

_____

_____

_____

_____

_____

_____

_____

Today's prayer:

_____

_____

_____

_____

_____

_____

_____

DAY 18

"Heaven's glow from you abounds"

What do I believe about this TRUTH?

_____

_____

_____

_____

_____

_____

_____

_____

_____

_____

_____

_____

_____

_____

_____

_____

_____

_____

_____

_____

_____

"Heaven's glow from you abounds"

What is my response to the revelation of HIS TRUTH?

_____

_____

_____

_____

_____

_____

_____

_____

_____

_____

_____

_____

_____

Today's prayer:

_____

_____

_____

_____

_____

_____

_____

What do I believe about this TRUTH?

_____

_____

_____

_____

_____

_____

_____

_____

_____

_____

_____

_____

_____

_____

_____

_____

_____

_____

_____

_____

What is my response to the revelation of HIS TRUTH?

_____

_____

_____

_____

_____

_____

_____

_____

_____

_____

_____

_____

Today's prayer: _____

_____

_____

_____

_____

_____

_____

DAY 20
"And you are beautiful"

What do I believe about this TRUTH?

_____
_____
_____
_____
_____
_____
_____
_____
_____
_____
_____
_____
_____
_____
_____
_____
_____
_____
_____
_____
_____
_____

What is my response to the revelation of HIS TRUTH?

_____

_____

_____

_____

_____

_____

_____

_____

_____

_____

_____

_____

Today's prayer:

_____

_____

_____

_____

_____

_____

62

You are righteous
Saved and sanctified
Forgiven, justified
You are righteous
And you are beautiful

DAY 21
"You are righteous"

What do I believe about this TRUTH?

_____

_____

_____

_____

_____

_____

_____

_____

_____

_____

_____

_____

_____

_____

_____

_____

_____

_____

_____

_____

What is my response to the revelation of HIS TRUTH?

_____

_____

_____

_____

_____

_____

_____

_____

_____

_____

_____

_____

Today's prayer:

_____

_____

_____

_____

_____

_____

_____

What do I believe about this TRUTH?

_____

_____

_____

_____

_____

_____

_____

_____

_____

_____

_____

_____

_____

_____

_____

_____

_____

_____

_____

_____

_____

What is my response to the revelation of HIS TRUTH?

_____

_____

_____

_____

_____

_____

_____

_____

_____

_____

_____

_____

Today's prayer:

_____

_____

_____

_____

_____

_____

What do I believe about this TRUTH?

_____

_____

_____

_____

_____

_____

_____

_____

_____

_____

_____

_____

_____

_____

_____

_____

_____

_____

_____

_____

What is my response to the revelation of HIS TRUTH?

_____

_____

_____

_____

_____

_____

_____

_____

_____

_____

_____

Today's prayer:

_____

_____

_____

_____

_____

_____

_____

DAY 24
"You are righteous"

What do I believe about this TRUTH?

_____

_____

_____

_____

_____

_____

_____

_____

_____

_____

_____

_____

_____

_____

_____

_____

_____

_____

_____

_____

_____

What is my response to the revelation of HIS TRUTH?

_____

_____

_____

_____

_____

_____

_____

_____

_____

_____

_____

_____

_____

Today's prayer:

_____

_____

_____

_____

_____

_____

_____

What do I believe about this TRUTH?

_____

_____

_____

_____

_____

_____

_____

_____

_____

_____

_____

_____

_____

_____

_____

_____

_____

_____

_____

_____

_____

_____

What is my response to the revelation of HIS TRUTH?

_____

_____

_____

_____

_____

_____

_____

_____

_____

_____

_____

_____

Today's prayer:

_____

_____

_____

_____

_____

_____

_____

74

You are redeemed
The Lamb was crucified
For you, the Savior died
You are redeemed
And you are beautiful

DAY 26
"You are redeemed"

What do I believe about this TRUTH?

_____

_____

_____

_____

_____

_____

_____

_____

_____

_____

_____

_____

_____

_____

_____

_____

_____

_____

_____

_____

_____

What is my response to the revelation of HIS TRUTH?

_____

_____

_____

_____

_____

_____

_____

_____

_____

_____

_____

_____

Today's prayer:

_____

_____

_____

_____

_____

_____

_____

DAY 27
"The Lamb was crucified"

What do I believe about this TRUTH?

_____

_____

_____

_____

_____

_____

_____

_____

_____

_____

_____

_____

_____

_____

_____

_____

_____

_____

_____

_____

_____

What is my response to the revelation of HIS TRUTH?

_____

_____

_____

_____

_____

_____

_____

_____

_____

_____

_____

Today's prayer:

_____

_____

_____

_____

_____

_____

_____

What do I believe about this TRUTH?

_____

_____

_____

_____

_____

_____

_____

_____

_____

_____

_____

_____

_____

_____

_____

_____

_____

_____

_____

_____

_____

_____

"For you, the Savior died"

What is my response to the revelation of HIS TRUTH?

_____

_____

_____

_____

_____

_____

_____

_____

_____

_____

_____

_____

Today's prayer:

_____

_____

_____

_____

_____

_____

_____

"You are redeemed"

What do I believe about this TRUTH?

_____

_____

_____

_____

_____

_____

_____

_____

_____

_____

_____

_____

_____

_____

_____

_____

_____

_____

_____

_____

What is my response to the revelation of HIS TRUTH?

_____

_____

_____

_____

_____

_____

_____

_____

_____

_____

_____

_____

_____

Today's prayer:

_____

_____

_____

_____

_____

_____

DAY 30
"And you are beautiful"

What do I believe about this TRUTH?

_____

_____

_____

_____

_____

_____

_____

_____

_____

_____

_____

_____

_____

_____

_____

_____

_____

_____

_____

_____

_____

_____

"And you are beautiful"

What is my response to the revelation of HIS TRUTH?

_____

_____

_____

_____

_____

_____

_____

_____

_____

_____

_____

_____

Today's prayer: _____

_____

_____

_____

_____

_____

_____

_____

86

You are purity
Darkness turned to light
Perfect in His sight
You are purity
And you are beautiful

DAY 31
"You are purity"

What do I believe about this TRUTH?

_____

_____

_____

_____

_____

_____

_____

_____

_____

_____

_____

_____

_____

_____

_____

_____

_____

_____

_____

_____

What is my response to the revelation of HIS TRUTH?

_____

_____

_____

_____

_____

_____

_____

_____

_____

_____

_____

_____

Today's prayer:

_____

_____

_____

_____

_____

_____

_____

DAY 32
"Darkness turned to light"

What do I believe about this TRUTH?

_____

_____

_____

_____

_____

_____

_____

_____

_____

_____

_____

_____

_____

_____

_____

_____

_____

_____

_____

_____

_____

"Darkness turned to light"

What is my response to the revelation of HIS TRUTH?

_____

_____

_____

_____

_____

_____

_____

_____

_____

_____

_____

_____

_____

Today's prayer:

_____

_____

_____

_____

_____

_____

_____

What do I believe about this TRUTH?

_____

_____

_____

_____

_____

_____

_____

_____

_____

_____

_____

_____

_____

_____

_____

_____

_____

_____

_____

_____

_____

What is my response to the revelation of HIS TRUTH?

_____

_____

_____

_____

_____

_____

_____

_____

_____

_____

_____

_____

_____

Today's prayer:

_____

_____

_____

_____

_____

_____

_____

DAY 34
"You are purity"

What do I believe about this TRUTH?

_____

_____

_____

_____

_____

_____

_____

_____

_____

_____

_____

_____

_____

_____

_____

_____

_____

_____

_____

_____

_____

_____

_____

_____

What is my response to the revelation of HIS TRUTH?

_____

_____

_____

_____

_____

_____

_____

_____

_____

_____

_____

_____

Today's prayer:

_____

_____

_____

_____

_____

_____

_____

DAY 35
"And you are beautiful"

What do I believe about this TRUTH?

_____

_____

_____

_____

_____

_____

_____

_____

_____

_____

_____

_____

_____

_____

_____

_____

_____

_____

_____

_____

_____

"And you are beautiful"

What is my response to the revelation of HIS TRUTH?

_____

_____

_____

_____

_____

_____

_____

_____

_____

_____

_____

_____

Today's prayer:

_____

_____

_____

_____

_____

_____

_____

98

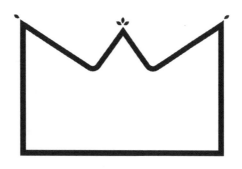

You are a child of God
Beloved and so adored
Treasured by our Lord
You are a child of God
And you are beautiful

What do I believe about this TRUTH?

_____

_____

_____

_____

_____

_____

_____

_____

_____

_____

_____

_____

_____

_____

_____

_____

_____

_____

_____

_____

_____

What is my response to the revelation of HIS TRUTH?

_____

_____

_____

_____

_____

_____

_____

_____

_____

_____

_____

_____

_____

Today's prayer:

_____

_____

_____

_____

_____

_____

_____

DAY 37
"Beloved and so adored"

What do I believe about this TRUTH?

_____

_____

_____

_____

_____

_____

_____

_____

_____

_____

_____

_____

_____

_____

_____

_____

_____

_____

_____

_____

_____

What is my response to the revelation of HIS TRUTH?

_____

_____

_____

_____

_____

_____

_____

_____

_____

_____

_____

_____

Today's prayer:

_____

_____

_____

_____

_____

_____

DAY 38
"Treasured by our Lord"

What do I believe about this TRUTH?

_____

_____

_____

_____

_____

_____

_____

_____

_____

_____

_____

_____

_____

_____

_____

_____

_____

_____

_____

_____

_____

"Treasured by our Lord"

What is my response to the revelation of HIS TRUTH?

_____

_____

_____

_____

_____

_____

_____

_____

_____

_____

_____

_____

Today's prayer:

_____

_____

_____

_____

_____

_____

_____

"You are a child of God"

What do I believe about this TRUTH?

_____

_____

_____

_____

_____

_____

_____

_____

_____

_____

_____

_____

_____

_____

_____

_____

_____

_____

_____

_____

_____

_____

What is my response to the revelation of HIS TRUTH?

_____

_____

_____

_____

_____

_____

_____

_____

_____

_____

_____

_____

Today's prayer:

_____

_____

_____

_____

_____

_____

_____

DAY 40
"And you are beautiful"

What do I believe about this TRUTH?

_____

_____

_____

_____

_____

_____

_____

_____

_____

_____

_____

_____

_____

_____

_____

_____

_____

_____

_____

_____

_____

_____

"And you are beautiful"

What is my response to the revelation of HIS TRUTH?

_____

_____

_____

_____

_____

_____

_____

_____

_____

_____

_____

_____

Today's prayer:

_____

_____

_____

_____

_____

_____

_____

110

Reflection

112

REFLECTION

Day 40 was a nice summary of my entire journey. My experience allowed God to reveal truths about the beginning of my life to present day. He led me in a magnificent way to the perfect word in the Bible or the perfect lyrics in a song to silence the lies from the enemy, and speak to my heart about His Truth. I am not who the enemy says I am, but I am who God says I am.

Day 40　　　　　　　*"And You Are Beautiful"*　　　　　　　**7.21.2016**

"This journey has brought me full circle, and has answered so many questions. It has brought me to my knees, to tears, and to rejoicing. My Father has revealed His Truth to me; His Truth about my life, from birth to current day when He reaffirmed my destiny. I had to take this 40 day journey to fully believe who I am in Christ before He could fully use me for others.

He found me, cleansed me, loved me, forgave me, and gave me a purpose. Through this journey, He has prepared me for ministry, and has given me a new name, Segullah, meaning Treasured Possession."

My Prayer Today: "Thank you Heavenly Father for your everlasting love. You are my Abba Father who will never leave me nor forsake me. You are everything to me, and I will continue living the rest of my life to honor You and make You known – to be a true reflection of You, and *You Are Beautiful.*"

You have just read the last journal entry and prayer from my Day 40. Like I've said before, everyone's journey will be different. Did you experience great revelation through God's Truth? Were you set free from the lies you were believing? Did God confirm what you already believe? Did He speak to you about your purpose?

Please reflect on your 40 day journey experience and include your personal prayer on the next two pages.

_____

_____

_____

_____

_____

_____

_____

_____

_____

_____

_____

_____

_____

_____

_____

_____

_____

_____

_____

_____

_____

_____

_____

_____

_____

_____

_____

_____

_____

_____

_____

_____

_____

My personal prayer:

_____

_____

_____

_____

_____

_____

_____

116

Creative Pages

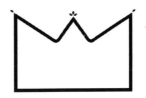

122

124

But you are a chosen people, a Royal priesthood.

1 PETER 2:9

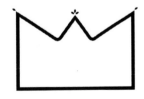

126

128

blessed are the PURE in heart, for they shall see God.

matthew 5:8

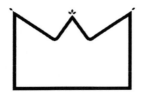

See what great
LOVE the
father
HAS LAVISHED
ON US, THAT WE
SHOULD BE CALLED
children
God.
1 John 3:11

134

References

REFERENCES FROM THE HOLY BIBLE

John 10:10

The thief comes only in order to steal and kill and destroy. I came that they may have *and* enjoy life, and have it in abundance [to the full, till it overflows].

John 1:17

For the law was given through Moses; grace and truth came through Jesus Christ.

John 8:32

Then you will know the truth, and the truth will set you free.

Romans 6:4

We were therefore buried with him through baptism into death in order that, just as Christ was raised from the dead through the glory of the Father, we too may live a new life.

Matthew 4:1-11

Then Jesus was led by the Spirit into the wilderness to be tempted by the devil. After fasting forty days and forty nights, he was hungry. The tempter came to him and said, "If you are the Son of God, tell these stones to become bread."

Jesus answered, "It is written: 'Man shall not live on bread alone, but on every word that comes from the mouth of God.'"

Then the devil took him to the holy city and had him stand on the highest point of the temple. "If you are the Son of God," he said, "throw yourself down. For it is written:

"'He will command his angels concerning you,
   and they will lift you up in their hands,
   so that you will not strike your foot against a stone.'"

Jesus answered him, "It is also written: 'Do not put the Lord your God to the test.'"

Again, the devil took him to a very high mountain and showed him all the kingdoms of the world and their splendor. "All this I will give you," he said, "if you will bow down and worship me."

Jesus said to him, "Away from me, Satan! For it is written: 'Worship the Lord your God, and serve him only.'"

Then the devil left him, and angels came and attended him.

Exodus 34:28-35

When Moses came down from Mount Sinai with the two tablets of the covenant law in his hands, he was not aware that his face was radiant because he had spoken with the LORD. When Aaron and all the Israelites saw Moses, his face was radiant, and they were afraid to come near him. But Moses called to them; so Aaron and all the leaders of the community came back to him, and he spoke to them. Afterward all the Israelites came near him, and he gave them all the commands the LORD had given him on Mount Sinai.

When Moses finished speaking to them, he put a veil over his face. But whenever he entered the LORD's presence to speak with him, he removed the veil until he came out. And when he came out and told the Israelites what he had been commanded, they saw that his face was radiant. Then Moses would put the veil back over his face until he went in to speak with the LORD.

For more information please visit

YouAreBeautifulSelah.com

Made in the USA
Middletown, DE
22 December 2017